Vocal Solos
For Communion and Lent Worship

THE COMMUNION SOLOIST

Table of Contents

FOREWORD

One of the most moving times within a communion service can be the singing of a solo while the elements are served. Since most churches celebrate communion at least several times a year, (some observe communion weekly) finding new, fresh, and appropriate solo literature can be difficult. Of course the idea is to support the subjective and introspective mood of the service with a solo that is warm and sensitive. Now is *not* the time for a display of vocal technique!

In my own church, I have found *The Cross Was His Own* to be wonderfully satisfying at the beginning of the serving of the elements. Perhaps the choir could sing a short communion hymn or chorale (preferably a cappella) followed by the soloist's selection. Also effective at this beginning time of the service would be *Lamb of God, What Wonderous Love, When I Survey the Wondrous Cross,* or *Come Share the Lord.* These pieces certainly set the mood for meditating on Christ's atoning death.

For a Maundy Thursday or Good Friday service, I know you will find the drama of *The Tree* extremely effective and suitable (this piece has an especially captivating accompaniment that works best on piano, not organ). And *Pie Jesu,* from the Fauré *Requiem,* is always welcome. Thomas Matthews' setting *The Lord is My Shepherd,* long a choral classic, is presented here in a vocal solo setting that is both strong and sensitive. For a more folk-style selection, try *Surely He Bore Our Griefs,* or Bryan Jeffery Leech's *Come Share the Lord.*

Vocal solos are most effective when memorized so that the singer can convincingly communicate the truths of the lyrics to the congregation (especially if you are seen when you sing!). I hope that you will find these pieces to be useful and challenging; and that the words and the music will be a source of comfort and remembrance to those who listen.

Fred Bock
Los Angeles, 1989

The Cross Was His Own

Unknown

Marjorie Jones

4

Lamb of God, What Wondrous Love

Words by
Russell A. Kane and
Allan Robert Petker

Based on "Pavane" by
Gabriel Fauré
Arranged by Allan Robert Petker

Here, O Lord, am I, fear - ful, sin - ful, man,

guil - ty and con - demned, Thy death is sure - ly mine.

Cross _____ of God, _____ I would to turn a - way, _____ yet

Love it bids me stay, O my soul.

Can it be the ver-y death I fear is that which draws me near, Lord, to Thee? Lamb of God, Thou died for me. Lamb of God, Thou died for me. Lamb of God, what won-drous love.

The Lord is My Shepherd

Psalm 23

Thomas Matthews

Available in sheet music, High Voice - F0103, Low Voice - F0113, published by H. T. FitzSimons Company.

right-eous-ness for His name's_ sake.____

Yea, though I walk through the val-ley of the sha-dow of death,

I will fear no e-vil: For Thou art with me; Thy

rod and Thy staff they com-fort me, they com-fort_ me,__ they com-fort_

all the days of my life: and I will

dwell,_ I will dwell_ in the house_ of the Lord for -

broaden

ev - - - er,   for - ev -

mp   *p*

Fr. Hn.

- - er. _____

Oboe

pp

When I Survey the Wondrous Cross

Words by
Isaac Watts

Music By
Lyn Murray

Did e'er such love and sor-row meet? or thorns com-pose so rich a crown? Were the whole realm of na-ture mine, that were an off-'ring far too small. Love so a-maz-ing, so di-vine,_____ De-mands my soul, my life, my all!_____

Manuals

Pedal

no breath

mp

The Tree

Words and Music By
Douglas Drobish
Arranged by Fred Bock

man him-self, the Tree more than a tree._____ *Slowly*

A

car-pen-ter the day He lived, He worked with wood in hand; The

Tree ___ a sym-bol of His work, a work great-er than man.___

So they stood there ___ side by side,___ just to let ___ the whole world

*Play this figure quickly but at accompanist's discretion.

Surely He Bore Our Griefs

Isaiah 53:4-6

David De Vidal

Come Share the Lord

Words and Music By
Bryan Jeffery Leech
Arranged by Roland Tabell

come drink the wine, come share the Lord.
come drink the wine, come share the

We'll gath-er

Lord. For He will feed us with His pres-ence here, this bread and

wine will do us good. Our deep-est hun-gers He will sat-is-fy, for He is

*Optional: You may replace the word "wine" with "cup" throughout the piece.

Pie Jesu
(Blessed Jesus)

English text and editing by
Mack Evans

Gabriel Fauré